Great MEALS

Great SNACKS

CHAPTERS BY: Jeanine Barone, MS; Betty Jean Carter, MS; Lisa Cohn, MMSc, RD; Donna Cross, GDHS; Arlene Spark, EdD, RD; Christine L. Williams, MD; Ernst L. Wynder, MD

EDITED BY: Joseph Wilkinson and the staff of Scholastic Inc.

DESIGNED BY: Joanne Slattery

PRODUCTION BY: Michael Tomassi

Findings on the causes and effects of children's blood cholesterol levels are from the American Health Foundation monograph, *Coronary Artery Disease Prevention: Cholesterol, a Pediatric Perspective.*

Great KIDS

Dear Parent:

By far, the most valuable gift we can give our children and ourselves is the gift of health. By promoting healthy family eating habits, we can actively improve our children's chances of living long, productive, healthy lives.

Over the past 20 years, the American Health Foundation has identified causes of certain diseases and developed ways to prevent such diseases. Research findings, including many from our labs and offices, link lifestyle to some of the more common diseases in the U.S. today. Lifestyle includes eating patterns, smoking or not, and personal health habits.

The impact of eating habits on lifelong health is the primary concern of this guide. Recently, studies of children's blood cholesterol levels have indicated that high cholesterol early in life is a risk factor for the later development of coronary artery disease and, ultimately, heart attack.

The average blood cholesterol level of children in the United States is too high. We recommend that each child's cholesterol level be tested. If that level is over 140, eating patterns should be changed to reduce the intake of saturated fat and cholesterol. The amount of saturated fat eaten daily should not exceed 11 grams for each 1,000 calories. The amount of cholesterol consumed should not be more than 300 milligrams per day.

This guide to healthful, nutritious eating is based on American Health Foundation findings contained in a scientific monograph on coronary-artery disease prevention released in June 1989. The guide contains low-fat, low-cholesterol menus and recipes designed for you, the concerned parent. Suggestions in this book can improve your children's eating habits and reduce their risks of coronary-artery disease in later life.

As a nonprofit institute, the American Health Foundation conducts research and applies the results to public health education. One primary goal of the Foundation is to equip children to take responsibility for their health behaviors. We sincerely hope that children from age two on will become involved in healthful meal planning, shopping, and food preparation activities. In this way, they can give themselves, and in time their children, the gift of good health.

Ernst L. Wynder, M. D.
President
American Health Foundation

CONTENTS

1859829

Marti Shohet

HEARTS AT RISK

One out of every three children born this year is likely to have a serious heart attack or stroke before the age of 60.

Stephen Osborn

The major culprit? High blood cholesterol.

Children as young as two can begin to develop high blood cholesterol. Too much cholesterol in their blood leads to a gradual buildup of fatty deposits on the walls of the arteries. During adulthood, this buildup can block arteries completely. The result can be a heart attack, a stroke, or some related disease.

Coronary artery disease, the blockage of arteries that feed blood to and from the heart, is the leading cause of death in the United States. Right now, about 5.4 million Americans suffer from coronary heart disease. During the coming year, one out of four in this group will suffer a heart attack. Of these 1.5 million heart attack victims, 350,000 will die before reaching the hospital.

Too much cholesterol in a person's blood over many years results in atherosclerosis, also known as "hardening of the arteries." According to

GRADUAL CLOGGING OF ARTERIES

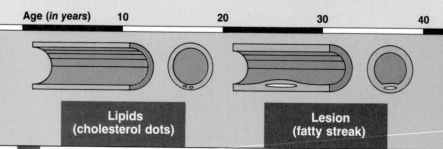

Age (*in years*)   10   20   30   40

Lipids
(cholesterol dots)

Lesion
(fatty streak)

Marti Shohet

studies by the American Health Foundation, tendencies toward hardening of the arteries begin in childhood. These early tendencies first became evident during examinations of the arteries of children who died in accidents. It was found that the higher the cholesterol levels, the greater the fatty deposits in the arteries. Recent tests indicate that one out of every four children in the U.S. has a cholesterol level that needs to be lowered. One in eight has a cholesterol level that poses a health risk.

Two factors, heredity and eating habits, contribute to high blood cholesterol in children. A child with high cholesterol might have a parent or other relative with high cholesterol levels. But most high cholesterol

Hardening of the arteries (atherosclerosis) may begin as deposits of fatty dots in childhood, setting the stage for clogging in later years.

50   60   70   80

Fibrous Plaque
(hardening fat)

Narrowed Artery
(danger of blockage)

A gram (g), the basic metric measure of mass and weight, is a small unit. Just 28.35 grams equal an ounce. On nutrition labels of packaged foods, *fat content* is usually given in *grams, cholesterol content* in *milligrams.*

A paperclip weighs about 1 gram.

Three aspirins weigh about 1 gram.

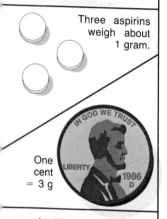

One cent = 3 g

A milligram (mg) is an extremely small unit.

One mosquito = 100mg

1,000 mg = 1 g

among children is caused by their eating food high in animal fat and cholesterol. High blood cholesterol isn't something that a child will grow out of. It stays high and increases with age, unless something is done about it.

THE GOOD NEWS: You can help your children keep their blood cholesterol at healthy levels. If their cholesterol levels are already high, you can help them lower those levels to healthy standards. These actions will increase your children's chances of avoiding coronary artery (cardiovascular) disease in later life.

Because high cholesterol tendencies start in childhood, this is the best time to try to prevent them. You can take two giant steps to help your children beat the threat of high cholesterol:

● **Have your children's blood cholesterol checked by a doctor at regular intervals.** This is a simple test for a child, requiring just a few drops of blood taken by pricking a finger. It doesn't cost much and can be made part of a regular physical exam.

● **Make some easy adjustments in the food that your children eat.** These changes can set lifetime healthful eating habits.

DANGERS AHEAD

Hardening and thickening of the arteries can lead to dangerous health conditions.

Occlusion (blockage) of an artery supplying blood to the heart muscle is a common cause of death.

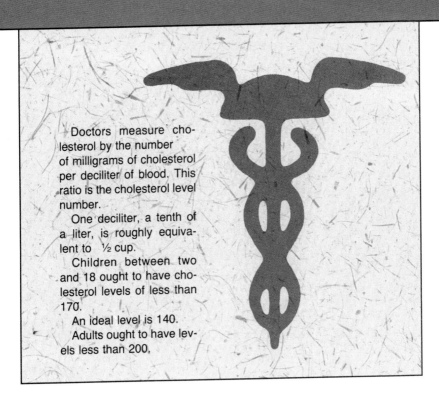

Doctors measure cholesterol by the number of milligrams of cholesterol per deciliter of blood. This ratio is the cholesterol level number.

One deciliter, a tenth of a liter, is roughly equivalent to ½ cup.

Children between two and 18 ought to have cholesterol levels of less than 170.

An ideal level is 140.

Adults ought to have levels less than 200.

Although cholesterol buildup in the arteries is a menacing condition, it can usually be reversed and controlled by good eating habits. The following pages will show you how to lower your children's cholesterol levels by helping them to eat in a healthy way.

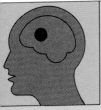

lockage of the flow of lood to the brain can ause a stroke.

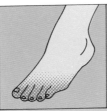

A reduction in the flow of blood to fingers and toes causes tingling, cramps, numbness and, in severe cases, gangrene (death of local tissue).

Hardening can lead to an aneurysm (ballooning of artery) which can result in a burst blood vessel.

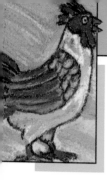

WHAT FOOD IS ALL ABOUT

Stephen Osborn

Food is made up of six components: fat, protein, carbohydrates, vitamins, minerals and water.

Most foods are combinations of the first five components, plus water.

Food is our bodies' fuel. We need it for everything we do: breathing, eating, walking, talking, running, jumping, even

NUTRIENTS IN BASIC FOODS

Meat and fish contain protein, fat, vitamins and minerals, but little carbohydrate.

Breads and cereals have carbohydrates, protein, vitamins, minerals and small amounts of fat.

Vegetables contain carbohydrates, protein, vitamins and minerals, and little fat. **Fruits** are similar but have much less protein. Avocados, olives and nuts, however, contain an amount of fat.

Eggs and dairy products contain protein, fat, vitamins and minerals, but little carbohydrate.

sleeping. The fuel we don't use up each day is stored in our bodies as fat.

The fuel value of food is measured in calories, or units of energy. The caloric value of foods varies. A 100-gram brownie contains more calories than 100 grams of lettuce.

Foods are mixtures of protein, fat and carbohydrates. We need all three, but as the following chapters show, the proportions we need of each are different.

Fats and oils, such as butter, lard, olive oil and corn oil, contain fat and small amounts of vitamins and minerals, but no protein or carbohydrates.

Sugar consists only of carbohydrate.

FATS HAVE MORE CALORIES

Calories per gram

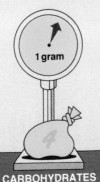

CARBOHYDRATES
1 gram = 4 calories

PROTEIN
1 gram = 4 calories

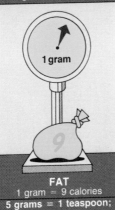

FAT
1 gram = 9 calories
5 grams = 1 teaspoon;
28 grams = 1 ounce

FAT AND CHOLESTEROL

Stephen Osborn

The villains linked to coronary heart disease are fat and cholesterol. Like most villains, neither one is *all* bad.

Cholesterol is a natural substance. Your body produces it to make hormones, cell membranes and insulation for nerves.

Fat, too, is natural to the body and useful. It transports vitamins, shields the brain from harmful chemicals, provides body insulation, and cushions

Marti Shohet

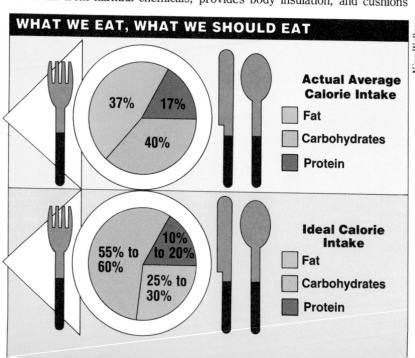

WHAT WE EAT, WHAT WE SHOULD EAT

Actual Average Calorie Intake
- Fat — 37%
- Carbohydrates — 40%
- Protein — 17%

Ideal Calorie Intake
- Fat — 10% to 20%
- Carbohydrates — 55% to 60%
- Protein — 25% to 30%

Nina Wallace

some vital organs. We need to consume some fat each day to stay healthy.

Like most things in life, though, a little is good, but too much is harmful. Our livers can make all the cholesterol that our bodies need. Although we need to get some fat from the food we eat, we don't need as much as most of us get every day.

Americans tend to eat too much fat. We get almost 40 percent of our calories from fat. To reduce the risk of clogging our arteries, we should cut that down to less than 30 percent.

There are basically two kinds of fat: saturated fat (which should be limited) and unsaturated fat. We get saturated fat from meat, eggs and dairy foods, such as milk, cheese, butter and ice cream. Palm oil and coconut oil also contain saturated fat. Unsaturated fat, the better kind, comes from plants. Unsaturated fats include olive oil, peanut oil, corn oil, safflower and sunflower seed oil.

To help you control the amounts of fat and cholesterol your children eat, discover how dietitians measure these substances. You will be able to keep track of the amounts of fat and cholesterol in food, and you will also be better equipped to understand the content labels on packaged foods.

FAT FACTS

Almost 40 percent of the calories consumed by Americans are fats. This should be lowered to less than 30 percent of calories consumed.

There are three kinds of fat:
Saturated fat, which comes mostly from animal foods, raises cholesterol levels. It is usually solid at room temperature.
Monounsaturated fat includes olive oil and peanut oil. It is liquid at room temperature, and it helps lower cholesterol levels.
Polyunsaturated fat includes vegetable oils, such as corn oil and safflower oil. Unless it is hydrogenated (hydrogen added), it is liquid at room temperature. It helps lower cholesterol levels.

The more saturated fats your children eat, the more likely they are to develop high cholesterol. While their total fat intake should not exceed 30 percent, their saturated fat intake should not exceed 10 percent of calories consumed.

Cholesterol in food, the other villain, also raises blood cholesterol. You'll find it in meat, shrimp, eggs and dairy products.

WHAT'S IN A CUP OF MILK?

Protein

Whole	8 g
2%	8 g
1%	8 g
Skim	8 g

Fat

Whole	5 g
2%	3 g
1%	1.5 g
Skim	.3 g

Calcium

Whole	291 mg
2%	297 mg
1%	300 mg
Skim	302 mg

Cholesterol

Whole	33 mg
2%	22 mg
1%	10 mg
Skim	4 mg

Food components are measured in grams or milligrams. These are metric measurements of weight, which are used because all metric measures are divisible by 10.

The main components of food — fat, protein and carbohydrates — are measured in grams (g). Cholesterol and vitamins are measured in milligrams (mg). Ideally, your children shouldn't eat more than 300 mg of cholesterol a day (nearly the equivalent of the cholesterol in one egg yolk).

As you can see in the table on page 13, foods that are very high in cholesterol include liver, kidneys, brains, shrimp and eggs.

Hardly any child in the United States willingly eats liver, kidneys or brains. Shrimp is too expensive to eat a lot of. So that leaves eggs as the main high-cholesterol food.

Fatty food is the main cause of high cholesterol levels in children. You should see that your children get no more than 30 percent of their

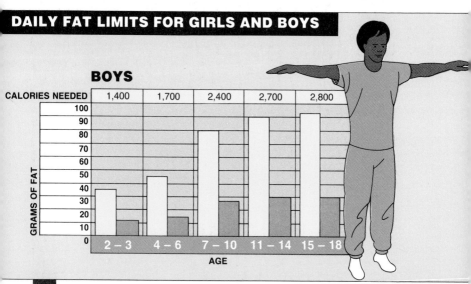

DAILY FAT LIMITS FOR GIRLS AND BOYS

BOYS

CALORIES NEEDED	1,400	1,700	2,400	2,700	2,800

GRAMS OF FAT (scale: 0 to 100)

AGE: 2 – 3   4 – 6   7 – 10   11 – 14   15 – 18

daily calories from fat. That applies to the total of both saturated and unsaturated fat. The amount of saturated fat should be no more than 10 percent of total calories eaten.

The table on this page tells you the recommended limits of total and saturated fat intake per day for boys and girls of different ages, on the basis of their recommended daily allowances of calories.

The tables in the back of this book will show you how much fat and cholesterol are in various food items. Also, many packaged foods carry nutrition information, including fat and cholesterol amounts.

In selecting foods, the main thing to watch out for is fat, especially saturated fat. Except for foods like eggs and liver, if you keep track of saturated fat, the cholesterol will take care of itself. For each child in your family, look up the saturated fat goal in the chart above, and make sure that he or she doesn't go over that goal.

SOME HIGH-CHOLESTEROL FOODS

shrimp (3 oz.) - 125 mg

egg (one) - 275 mg

liver (3 oz.) - 370 mg

kidneys (3 oz.) - 680 mg

brains (3 oz.) - 1,700 mg

□ Total fat limit (grams)
■ Saturated fat limit (grams)

GIRLS

CALORIES NEEDED	1,400	1,700	2,400	2,200	2,100

GRAMS OF FAT — scale: 0, 10, 20, 30, 40, 50, 60, 70, 80, 90, 100

AGE: 2 – 3   4 – 6   7 – 10   11 – 14   15 – 18

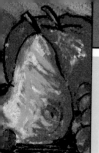

How to CUT BACK ON FAT

Reducing the fat your family eats is a challenge. Your best bet is to gradually cut back on fatty foods.

Stephen Osborn

A big source of fat is milk. A child of six who drinks three glasses of whole milk a day has already taken in two thirds of the ideal daily allowance of fat. The solution is to switch to skim milk or milk with 1 percent fat.

Although they make a lot of noise about changing the world, children are resistant to new things. They'll fight change just because it's change. If you want to get young children on skim or low-fat milk, do it gradually and don't tell them. Start them off with a mix of one-fourth skim and three-fourths whole milk. Over 10 days, gradually give them more skim or low-fat and less whole milk.

REDUCE MEAT FAT

Another big source of fat in your children's food is meat. You can cut down on the fat content by

WHERE THE SATURATED FATS ARE

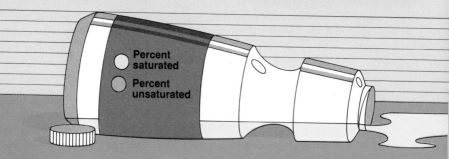

Percent saturated

Percent unsaturated

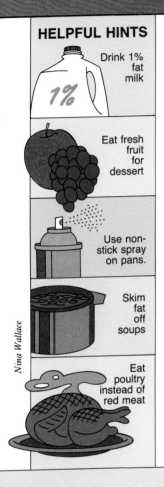

Drink 1% fat milk

Eat fresh fruit for dessert

Use non-stick spray on pans.

Skim fat off soups

Eat poultry instead of red meat

Nina Wallace

changing your ways of buying it and cooking it.

● Buy leaner cuts of meat. That will be easier not only on your children's arteries, but also on your budget. A beef rump roast is not only leaner than prime ribs of beef, but a lot cheaper.

● Chicken and turkey are not only leaner than beef, pork and lamb, but they also give you more protein for your dollar than other meats. You can make them leaner by serving the meat without the skin. Try to phase out fried chicken. Not only is it drenched in fat, but it can't easily be served without the skin. White-meat chicken or turkey is lower in fat than dark meat.

● Cut back on fried foods. This includes fried potatoes as well as fried meat and fish. Instead of frying, roast or broil the meat. Broil or bake fish. If you must fry, get a nonstick pan or a nonstick spray so that fat isn't needed.

● Trim the fat off meat before you cook it. Fat that is left on meat during cooking tends to penetrate the meat and stay in it.

● Remember, well-done meat has less fat than rare meat.

● Stews and casseroles can be cooked a day ahead of time and refrigerated. Before reheating, skim away the congealed fat on the surface.

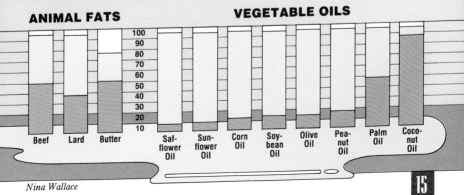

ANIMAL FATS **VEGETABLE OILS**

Beef Lard Butter Safflower Oil Sunflower Oil Corn Oil Soybean Oil Olive Oil Peanut Oil Palm Oil Coconut Oil

Nina Wallace

An easy way to reduce fat consumption is to serve occasional meatless meals, such as pasta with marinara sauce, rice and beans, eggplant stuffed with nuts and raisins, and vegetable stew.

THE FAT BETWEEN THE BREAD

Phase out processed meats. You can avoid giving your children a lot of useless fat and save money as well by eliminating bologna, salami, liver-wurst, frankfurters, sausages and ham loaf.

Take a look at the prices on these luncheon meats the next time you're in the supermarket. They cost about half again more per pound than unprocessed beef, veal, lamb and pork. They also often have 50 percent more fat in them than the leaner meats.

Processed meats are used almost entirely for making sandwiches. Cook your own sandwich meat. It will be not only healthier but also cheaper. Roast chicken, turkey, beef and pork. Bake or boil ham. Use these meats for sandwiches instead of luncheon meats.

If you're serving frankfurters, your best choice would be chicken or turkey hot dogs.

Almost every child loves hamburgers. If you're making them, be sure you use lean beef. Buy ground round, or even lean ground round. It has much less fat than ground chuck. Avoid buying what supermarkets call hamburger or ground beef. Federal regulations allow hamburger meat to contain 30 percent fat. When you buy this kind of meat you are either filling your child with life-threatening fat or draining off the fat and throwing away 30 cents out of every dollar you spend on it. Many people are now turning to the alternative of ground turkey burgers.

EACH GROUP CONTAINS

2 cups of whole milk

2 slices American cheese

1 scoop of ice cream

DON'T LEAVE HOME WITHOUT A PLAN

The secret of preparing low-fat meals that your family will enjoy is meal planning. Before you go shopping, talk about the low-fat foods your family is willing to try. Prepare a shopping list with low-fat options for the food items you plan to buy. In the store, read the labels. Buy only what you need. Don't buy food because you think it might come in handy. Don't stock up on meat or dairy food for snacks. There are plenty of non-fat foods to snack on, as you'll see later in this guide to healthful eating.

DON'T MAKE EVERY DAY THANKSGIVING

Family-style service, or putting all the food that has been prepared for dinner out on the table, is an American tradition. Parents like to feel that they can provide abundant tables for their families and allow each person to take as much as he or she wants. The problem is that by encouraging people to take large helpings and second helpings, family-style service often leads to overeating.

Phase out fat by switching to plate service. Portion the food onto each person's plate in the the kitchen. Leave no second helpings of fatty

NOW YOU SEE IT, NOW YOU DON'T....

Added (Visible) Fats (Oily or creamy to touch)
salad oils
butter
margarine
sour cream
mayonnaise
creamy cheese

Built-in (Invisible) Fats (Usually not oily until heated)
marbling in meat
poultry skin
bacon
nuts
hard cheeses
creamy candy bars

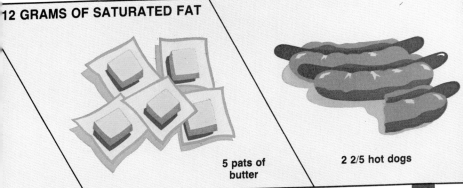

12 GRAMS OF SATURATED FAT

5 pats of butter

2 2/5 hot dogs

foods in sight and don't offer any. Your family might rebel at an overnight introduction of plate service. You could phase it in initially by putting just meat on plates in the kitchen and leaving vegetables in serving bowls on the table.

Make large salads and low-fat vegetable dishes. Serve whole-grain or whole-wheat bread. If a spread is needed, provide jams and peanut butter instead of butter or margarine.

THE SWEET ENDING

Probably the biggest challenge you'll have with reducing fat is in the serving of desserts. The desserts children like best are cake, pie and ice cream, which are all loaded with fat.

Store-bought baked goods are heavy in fat. You can phase out a lot of fat by making your own desserts from recipes in this book. You can also serve sherbets, ice milk, or frozen-fruit bars instead of ice cream.

Stop buying ice cream by the gallon and storing it in the freezer. Try to limit your ice cream purchases and then buy only enough for one meal. Make ice cream a special treat, not a staple.

The perfect dessert for your children's health is fresh fruit. It's also the perfect snack. Keep a variety of fruit in the house. Take fruit snacks with you when you go out with your children. There's hardly an ounce of fat or cholesterol in a ton of apples or a carload of oranges or a roomful of bananas.

INVOLVE YOUR CHILDREN

Children can usually identify fatty foods as being greasy, creamy or oily. Show them greasy droplets on plates that held meat or cheese dishes. Show them the solid fat that forms on refrigerated meat stews and soups.

However, children should be aware that some greasy, creamy or oily foods are less desirable than others. Teach your children to identify where a food comes from. Is it an animal food or a vegetable food? This will enable them to determine whether the food has a lot of saturated fat and cholesterol. In general, animal foods contain more saturated fat than plant foods. And *only animal foods contain cholesterol.*

Explain to your children that low-fat or no-fat foods should be eaten often while high-fat foods should be eaten rarely. Include your children in making food decisions. You can encourage them to make shopping lists.

LIFETIME EATING

Remember, the way to a healthy life for your children is development of eating habits that will last a lifetime. You aren't setting up a diet. Diets are something that people go on for a short time and don't like anyway. When they give them up, they go back to the wrong eating that made them fat or threatened their health in the first place.

You don't have to create good eating habits for your family overnight. Good food strategies work best if you phase them in quietly and gradually.

Make an effort to have your family eat together as often as possible. It gives you more control over your children's eating habits. In the long run, it's good for their hearts.

Young Children Can Be Fatty-Food Detectives

Activities to Identify Sources of Fat and Cholesterol

- Fatty foods are usually creamy, greasy or oily. Encourage your children to look at, touch and taste a food item to find out whether or not it is fatty.
- Show how butter and cream cheese become soft and creamy at room temperature.
- Point out that greasy foods (French fries, potato chips, butter rolls) leave oily stains on brown paper bags.
- Have your children list their favorite foods. Help them identify fatty foods.

Involvement Projects

- Help your children list low-fat options for many of the fatty foods they like.
- Make up colorful certificates to encourage your kids to make healthful choices. Here's an example:

My Lunch Choices	Vegetables I Tried
1. Tuna Salad	1. Broccoli
2.	2.
3.	3.

PHASE IN CARBOHYDRATES

Carbohydrates are your best friends when it comes to controlling the level of cholesterol in your children's blood. We have learned a lot about food in the past 30 years, but we haven't yet succeeded in unlearning some myths. As a result of fad diets of 30 years ago and even more recent times, carbohydrates have been mistakenly called dull and fattening.

There are two kinds of carbohydrates:

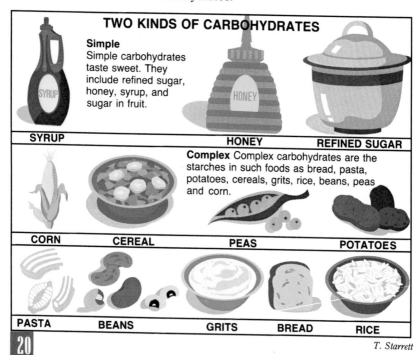

TWO KINDS OF CARBOHYDRATES

Simple
Simple carbohydrates taste sweet. They include refined sugar, honey, syrup, and sugar in fruit.

SYRUP | HONEY | REFINED SUGAR

Complex Complex carbohydrates are the starches in such foods as bread, pasta, potatoes, cereals, grits, rice, beans, peas and corn.

CORN | CEREAL | PEAS | POTATOES

PASTA | BEANS | GRITS | BREAD | RICE

T. Starrett

- **Simple carbohydrates** taste sweet. They include the different sugars that appear in our diet: table sugar, honey, and syrup. Such sugars provide energy, but nothing else. The sugar in fruits (fructose) and the sugar in milk (lactose) also provide energy, but the fruit and the milk also provide vitamins and minerals.
- **Complex carbohydrates** are all the starches we eat in the form of bread, pasta, potatoes, cereals, grains, rice, beans, peas, and corn. They are packed with vitamins and minerals.

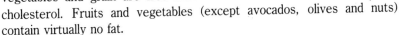

The easiest way to cut back on the amount of fat and cholesterol that your children eat is to feed them more complex carbohydrates. Fruit, vegetables and grain are free from cholesterol. Fruits and vegetables (except avocados, olives and nuts) contain virtually no fat.

Carbohydrate foods should make up more than half of the calories your children eat—at least 55 percent. Not only are they free of fat and cholesterol, they also provide dietary fiber — roughage.

Marti Shohet

GET FIBER WITH YOUR FOOD

■ Dietary fiber is found only in plant foods. It consists of complex carbohydrates that humans cannot digest.

■ Although we can't digest it, we need fiber in our food.

■ Dietary fiber is part of grains, fruits, vegetables, nuts and seeds.

■ There are two types of dietary fiber: *water insoluble* and *water soluble*. Insoluble fiber aids digestion. Soluble fiber plays a part in lowering blood cholesterol.

■ Many scientists consider that dietary fiber may help prevent colon cancer, diabetes and heart disease.

SOME FOODS RICH IN FIBER

Great Fiber Sources
Bran-rich cereal (1 oz.) . . . . . 8-10 g
Baked beans (½ cup) . . . . 9 g
Wheat germ (½ cup) . . . . 7 g
Kidney beans (½ cup) . . . . 7 g

Very Good Fiber Sources
Navy beans (½ cup) . . . . 6 g
Dried peas (½ cup) . . . . 5 g
Lima beans (½ cup) . . . . 5 g
Bran cereal (1 oz) . . . . 5 g

Good Fiber Sources
Apple with skin (1) . . . . 4 g
Peas (½ cup) . . . . 4 g
Lentils (½ cup) . . . . 4 g
Corn (½ cup) . . . . 3 g
Potato with skin (1) . . . . 3 g
Prunes (3) . . . . 3 g
Raspberries (½ cup) . . . . 3 g
Apricots (2) . . . . 2 g
Oatmeal (¾ cup) . . . . 2 g
Broccoli (½ cup) . . . . 2 g
Carrot (½ cup) . . . . 2 g

T. Starrett

How to READ LABELS

You can do a better job of protecting your children's arteries from cholesterol build-up if you know how to read and understand the nutrition information on packaged food. You'll also be able to get more food value for your dollars.

Many labels are indefinite about the kinds of fats used. Some say: "Contains one or more of the following: sunflower seed oil, coconut oil and/or palm oil." Sunflower seed oil is a better oil, because it is unsaturated. But palm oil and coconut oil are highly saturated.

Vegetable oils that have been hydrogenated or partially hydrogenated have saturated fat in them. Hydrogenation is the addition of hydrogen during processing. It makes an oily product solid or semisolid, increasing the saturated fat content. In buying margarine, look out for the words *hydrogenated* and *partially hydrogenated*. Choose margarine products that list liquid ingredients first.

The front of a food container, where the name and trademark are, will sometimes have brief descriptive labels, such as *low-calorie, low-fat*, and *cholesterol-free.*

However, these descriptive labels can be misleading. "Cholesterol-free" doesn't mean fat-free. You'll see "cholesterol-free" on foods that never had cholesterol in the first place, like corn oil or olive oil, which are totally fat. The aim in protecting your children's future health is to cut down on *all* fats.

Marti Shohet

A TYPICAL NUTRITION LABEL

Nutrition information on the labels of most packaged foods is organized in this way.

BREAKFAST CEREAL FOOD

NUTRITION INFORMATION

SERVING SIZE: 1 OZ.
(28.4 g, ABOUT 1 CUP)
SERVINGS PER PACKAGE: 12

	CEREAL	WITH ½ CUP VITAMINS A & D SKIM MILK
CALORIES	100	140*
PROTEIN	2 g	6 g
CARBOHYDRATE	24 g	30 g
FAT	0 g	0 g*
CHOLESTEROL	0 mg	0 mg*
SODIUM	290 mg	350 mg
POTASSIUM	35 mg	240 mg

PERCENTAGE OF U.S. RECOMMENDED DAILY ALLOWANCES (U.S. RDA)

PROTEIN	4	15
VITAMIN A	25	30
VITAMIN C	25	25
THIAMIN	50	50
RIBOFLAVIN	50	60
NIACIN	50	50
CALCIUM	**	15
IRON	10	10
VITAMIN D	10	25
VITAMIN B$_6$	50	50
FOLIC ACID	50	50

*WHOLE MILK SUPPLIES AN ADDITIONAL 30 CALORIES, 4 g FAT, AND 15 mg CHOLESTEROL.
**CONTAINS LESS THAN 2% OF THE U.S. RDA OF THIS NUTRIENT.

INGREDIENTS: CORN, SUGAR, SALT, MALT FLAVORING, CORN SYRUP, **VITAMINS AND IRON:** VITAMIN C (SODIUM ASCORBATE AND ASCORBIC ACID), NIACINAMIDE, IRON, VITAMIN B$_6$ (PYRIDOXINE HYDROCHLORIDE), VITAMIN B$_2$ (RIBOFLAVIN), VITAMIN B$_1$ (THIAMIN HYDROCHLORIDE), VITAMIN A (PALMITATE), FOLIC ACID, AND VITAMIN D.

Nutrition Information: Serving size (in ounces, grams, pieces, or cups) and the number of servings the package holds are listed first. Listed next are usually the amounts, per serving, of calories, protein, carbohydrates, fat, cholesterol, sodium and potassium. Note: Some high-fat foods often list unrealistically small servings to make the fat and calorie content of each serving appear low.

General information: This section often notes the amount of fat in the food without stating how much of that fat is saturated. You can usually get an idea of the amount of saturated fat by using these guidelines: Fat in dairy products is half saturated; fat in meat is one-third to one-half saturated; fat in poultry and baked goods is one-third saturated.

Percentage of U.S. Recommended Daily Allowances: This refers to U.S. government recommendations for the amounts of protein and various vitamins and minerals we need each day. It shows you what percentages of your daily needs of protein, vitamins and minerals (% U.S. RDA) a serving of the food contains.

Ingredients: These are listed by the order of their weight in the product, from most to least. If there is more enriched white flour than whole wheat in "whole-wheat" bread, the white flour must be listed first.

T. Starrett

Suppose there is
NO NUTRITION LABEL

A lot of food doesn't come in a box, can, jar or package, so it doesn't have a nutrition label. Meat, fish and poultry usually don't carry labels, but you can guide your shopping by the low-fat, medium-fat and high-fat listings here.

VERY LOW-FAT

Vegetables: Except for olives, vegetables contain almost no fat.
Fruit: Except for avocados, fruits contain practically no fat.
Sugar: No sugar in any form contains fat.

LOW-FAT

For the following foods, a four-ounce serving has 12 g of fat, including 2 to 6 g of saturated fat, and 20 to 30 mg of cholesterol.
Beef: USDA "Good" or "Choice" grades of lean beef, such as round, sirloin and flank steak, tenderloin and chipped beef.
Pork: Lean pork, such as fresh ham, canned, cured or boiled ham, Canadian bacon and tenderloin.
Veal: All cuts are lean, except for veal cutlets (ground or cubed).
Poultry: Chicken, turkey, Cornish hen, all without skin.
Fish: All fresh and frozen fish, crabs, lobster, scallops, shrimp, clams, oysters, tuna canned in water, herrings (uncreamed), canned sardines.
Wild game: Venison, rabbit, squirrel, pheasant and duck without skin.

MEDIUM-FAT

For the following foods, a four-ounce serving has 20 g of fat, including 6 to 10g of saturated fat, and 20 to 30 mg of cholesterol.

Beef: Most beef products are in this category. All ground beef, roasts (rib, chuck, rump), steak (cubed, Porterhouse, T-bone), and meat loaf.

Pork: Most pork products are in this category. Chops, loin roast, cutlets.

Veal: Cutlet (ground or cubed, but unbreaded).

Poultry: Chicken with skin, ground turkey, domestic duck or goose well drained of fat.

Fish: Tuna canned in oil and drained, canned salmon.

Lamb: Most lamb products are in this category. Chops, leg and roast.

HIGH-FAT

For the following foods, a four-ounce serving has 32 g of fat, including 10 to 16 g of saturated fat, and 20 to 30 mg of cholesterol.

Beef: Most USDA "Prime" cuts of beef, such as ribs and corned beef.

Pork: Spare ribs, ground pork, pork sausage (link or patty).

Lamb: Patties (ground lamb).

Fish: Any fried fish product.

Other: Luncheon meat, such as salami and bologna; sausage; frankfurters.

Dairy products are often but not always labeled. Most are based on whole milk, which has 8 g of fat per cup, of which 5 g are saturated fat.

Low-fat and **fat-free** dairy products have some or all of the fat removed. These products include low-fat cottage cheese and cheeses such as part-skim mozzarella and ricotta.

Full-fat dairy products, such as whole-milk yogurt and full-fat cheeses, have the same fat content as whole milk.

High-fat dairy products are those in which water has been removed or butterfat added. Examples are evaporated milk, cream cheese, butter and cheeses like Brie.

In the produce section, you can feel at ease shopping for your family. Fresh fruits and vegetables are cholesterol-free, and, except for olives and avocados, fat-free.

The LOW-FAT BREAKFAST

Start the day right with a good breakfast. Children usually need the body fuel that a good breakfast provides to help them cope with classwork. Some studies have shown that children who skip breakfast do less well in school than children who eat proper breakfasts.

Breakfast should provide your children with at least one-fourth of their daily food needs, and it should be balanced. That is, it should have a variety of food that supplies enough protein, carbohydrates, fiber (roughage), vitamins and minerals.

Cereal with skim or low-fat milk and a glass of fruit juice or a piece of fruit make a balanced breakfast.

You can reduce fat and cholesterol at breakfast in several ways:

• Choose low-fat dairy products, such as skim or 1 percent-fat milk, cheese and yogurt, instead of whole milk and regular cheese and yogurt.

• Use peanut butter, apple butter, or jam instead of butter or margarine.

• Give a child no more than three egg yolks a week. When you make eggs,

boil or poach them if possible. If you do fry them, use a nonstick pan.

● Use nonstick pans for pancakes.

You can help lower your children's cholesterol levels by increasing dietary fiber at breakfast and all other meals by making these changes:

● Choose fresh fruit or vegetables, instead of juice.

● Have your children eat apples, pears, and peaches with the skins on. Wash the fruit first.

● Choose whole-grain breads and cereals, especially those containing oats and oat bran.

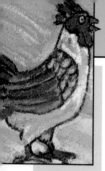

Seven
LOW-FAT BREAKFAST IDEAS

Stephen Osborn

You can schedule these breakfasts by the days of the week, or you can mix and match items from the different menus to provide interesting low-fat combinations. You can follow the same procedure with the lunch and dinner suggestions, which begin on pages 34 and 40. Asterisks indicate accompanying recipes.

1

*One serving of crisped rice cereal with
skim or 1 percent-fat milk
1 slice whole-wheat bread
1 tsp. jam
Banana berry smoothie**

2

Cereal yogurt breakfast crunch
1/2 banana, sliced
1 slice raisin toast
1 tsp. soft margarine
1 tsp. honey
1 cup low-fat milk*

3

Cheese omelette*
2 slices of rye toast, tablespoonful of applesauce
1 orange
1 cup low-fat milk

4

1 cup low-fat milk
1 serving of raisin bran
with skim or 1 percent-fat milk
Carrot bran muffin*
1 tsp. jam
1 tsp. soft margarine
6 ounces grape juice

5

Homemade granola*
1 apple
1 cup low-fat milk

6

French toast*
2 tsp. soft margarine
2 Tbsp. maple syrup
½ grapefruit
6 ounces pineapple juice

7

3 apple oatmeal pancakes*
2 tsp. soft margarine
Strawberries as topping
1 cup low-fat milk

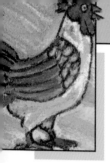

LOW-FAT BREAKFAST RECIPES

Stephen Osborn

BANANA BERRY SMOOTHIE   *2 Servings*

1 cup puréed strawberries   1 cup low-fat milk
1 large banana, sliced
Combine, blend, add ice cubes and serve cold.
Per Serving
Calories—169; Total Fat—12%; Sat. Fat—0.98 g; Choles.—5 mg; Fiber—5 g

CHEESE OMELETTE   *2 Servings*

6 egg whites   ½ small onion, chopped
3 Tbsp. low-fat cottage cheese   ½ green pepper, chopped
                                   1 Tbsp. olive oil
Sauté onion and pepper in oil. Beat egg whites and mix with cottage
cheese. Pour into hot frying pan. Add vegetables to center, fold in half, and
turn. Cook until golden.
Per Serving:
Calories—135; Total Fat—47%; Sat. Fat—1.12 g; Choles.—0.938 mg; Fiber—0.6 g

APPLE-OATMEAL PANCAKES   *6 Servings*

1 cup rolled oats, cooked   1 cup buttermilk
½ cup whole-wheat flour   2 egg whites
1 tsp. baking soda   1 Tbsp. apple juice
Combine all dry ingredients. In a separate small bowl, mix together the
milk, egg whites and apple juice. Stir this mixture into the dry ingredients.
Drop spoonfuls of the batter onto a hot, nonstick griddle. Cook until
golden—about one minute on each side.
Per Serving:
Calories—109; Total Fat—9%; Sat. Fat—0.2 g; Choles.—0; Fiber—2 g

CARROT MUFFIN

36 Muffins

1½ Tbsp. margarine
½ cup sugar
2 egg whites, whipped
2 cups buttermilk
1 cup raisins
½ cup molasses

2 cups grated carrots
1 cup white flour
1 cup whole-wheat flour
2 tsp. baking soda
¼ tsp. salt
¼ tsp. ginger

Preheat oven to 400° F.

Cream margarine with sugar. Add milk, raisins and molasses.

In a separate bowl, combine the flour, salt, baking soda and ginger. Stir the wet ingredients into the dry mixture. Fold in carrots and whipped egg whites. Bake for 15 minutes.

Per Muffin:
Calories—68.5; Total Fat—8%; Sat. Fat—0.11 g; Choles.—0; Fiber—1 g

HOMEMADE GRANOLA

4 Servings

2 cups rolled oats, uncooked
3 tsp. wheat germ
1 cup wheat flakes

1 cup raisins
1 tsp. cinnamon
1 tsp. nutmeg

Preheat oven to 450° F. Combine the ingredients. Spread the combination evenly on a cookie sheet. Bake for 5 minutes. Store in refrigerator.

Per Serving:
Calories—315; Total Fat—10%; Sat. Fat—0.73 g; Choles.—0; Fiber—7 g

FRENCH TOAST

4 Servings

4 slices whole-wheat bread
2 egg whites
¼ cup low-fat milk

¼ tsp. vanilla
¼ tsp. cinnamon
½ Tbsp. vegetable oil

Beat together egg whites, milk, vanilla and cinnamon. Dip bread in mixture and cook on oiled griddle. Allow about one minute for each side, or until each side is golden.

Per Serving:
Calories—76.1; Total Fat—15%; Sat. Fat—0.2 g; Choles.—0.625 mg; Fiber—2.83

CEREAL YOGURT BREAKFAST CRUNCH

1 Serving

1 cup low-fat vanilla yogurt
1 ounce cornflakes
Combine and serve.

2 tsp. brown sugar
½ banana, sliced

Per Serving:
Calories—447; Total Fat—7%; Sat. Fat—2.05 g; Choles.—11 mg; Fiber—3 g

The LOW-FAT LUNCH

A healthy, appetizing, attractive low-fat lunch is just as easy to prepare as one that is high in fat. Think lean. Be innovative.

Stephen Osborn

If your children aren't in school yet, your job is easy. You are in control of what they eat, if you wish to be. Preschool children are the easiest to introduce to low-fat eating. Remember, the more sensibly children eat at home, the more sensibly they'll eat away from home.

There are a number of *do's* and *don'ts* to keep in mind when it's time for school lunches.

Don't give your children lunch money. There's a lot of fat food waiting out there in the world of fast-food restaurants, vending machines, pizza parlors, school cafeterias, and candy stores.

Do prepare low-fat lunches for your school-age children. Sandwiches are children's favorite lunch food. It doesn't take much effort to make them low in fat. The best sandwich fillings are those you make yourself. Buy roast cuts of lean meat and trim off the visible fat. Roast beef, pork, veal, skinless chicken and turkey make appetizing meat sandwiches.

Don't give your children processed luncheon meats in sandwiches. These prepared meats — chopped ham, ham and cheese loaf, pimento loaf, liverwurst, bologna and salami — are loaded with fat and cholesterol.

Do think in terms of meatless sandwiches several times a week. Peanut butter is a strong favorite with most younger children. Canned tuna, either water-packed or well-drained of oil, and part-skim mozzarella and ricotta cheese can make nutritious, tasty sandwich fillings.

Don't use butter and mayonnaise as sandwich spreads. Both are high in fats and cholesterol. Ketchup, mustard, pickle relish and chutney have very little fat. Plain low-fat yogurt can be used instead of mayonnaise, not only as a sandwich spread, but also in making chicken and tuna salads.

Do use a variety of breads for sandwiches. There's not as much nutrition in white bread as in whole-grain breads. These sandwich breads taste good and have healthy fiber, vitamins and minerals. Try whole-wheat, rye, pumpernickel, wheat-berry, cracked-wheat, oat, and pita breads, as well as whole-grain flat bread and whole-wheat bagels.

Don't always choose your children's sandwiches for them. Get their ideas. Take them shopping with you and explain some low-fat alternatives. Let them help pack their own lunches.

School lunches don't have to be all sandwiches. Soup carried in a wide-mouth thermos makes a pleasant change. Any leftover vegetables can be pureed and combined with seasoning and broth to make a tasty, nutritious soup.

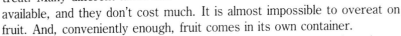

Fresh fruit is the best lunch treat. Many different kinds are available, and they don't cost much. It is almost impossible to overeat on fruit. And, conveniently enough, fruit comes in its own container.

Just about all the cookies, doughnuts, cakes and pies that are for sale are high in fat. If you have time, you can bake your children's favorite cookies using whole-wheat flour. Add oat bran for additional fiber.

The best drinks for your child's lunch are skim or 1 percent-fat milk and fruit juice.

Low-fat lunches are likely to be more of a problem if your children buy lunch in the school cafeteria. Get full information on what is served. Many school cafeterias are now increasing low-fat menu choices. Review school lunch menus with your children to identify low-fat items.

If your children have to rely on a fast-food restaurant for lunch, explain to them what high-fat food does to them. The younger the child, the more luck you'll have.

Fairly sensible eating in a fast-food restaurant is possible. A small hamburger is better for your children than a double or triple patty or a cheeseburger with bacon. A soda, because it has no fat, is better than a milk shake. A plain pizza or a regular pizza topped with vegetables is much better than a pizza with extra cheese, sausage, or pepperoni.

Marti Shohet

Stephen Osborn

Seven
LOW-FAT LUNCH IDEAS

1

Tomato, vegetable, rice soup
Taco with lean beef*
Salsa
Pear
Pineapple juice

2

BBQ chicken without skin
Oat muffin
Fruit salad
Gingersnaps
1 cup low-fat milk

3

Tuna salad* sandwich,
on pita bread
Carrot and bell pepper slices
Banana
1 cup low-fat milk

4

*Lean roast beef sandwich with
mustard, lettuce, tomato,
on cracked-wheat bread
Bean soup*
Apricot
Grapefruit juice*

5

*Cottage cheese sandwich with
tomato and cucumber slices,
on pumpernickel bread
Carrot salad with raisins
Berries
Banana shake**

6

*Turkey breast sandwich with
pineapple and celery,
on rye bread
½ baked sweet potato
Spice cookies*
Orange juice*

7

*Stuffed baked potato with egg white, broccoli and tomato
Salad with lettuce, cucumber, raisins and apples
Yogurt dressing*
Tangerine
1 cup low-fat milk*

Marti Shohet

Stephen Osborn

Low-Fat LUNCH RECIPES

TACO
4 Servings

¼ lb. very lean beef
⅛ cup chopped onions
¼ tsp. garlic, chopped
1 tsp. chili powder

¼ cups taco sauce
½ tsp. Dijon mustard
2 corn taco shells
¼ head lettuce, sliced
2 tomatoes, diced

Brown the meat in a nonstick pan. Combine onion, garlic, chili powder and mustard. Mix into the pan with the meat. Heat and stir for about one minute. Spoon into taco shells. Top with taco sauce and garnish with lettuce and tomato.

Per Serving:
Calories—125; Total Fat—46%; Sat. Fat—1.85 g; Choles.—23 mg; Fiber— 1.7 g

BEAN SOUP
8 Servings

12-ounce can of red kidney beans
    or black beans
15 ounces crushed tomatoes
3 cups water
1 onions, chopped

1 green pepper, chopped
1 Tbsp. garlic, chopped
1 Tbsp. olive oil
1 Tbsp. chili powder

Rinse beans and cook in water until tender. Add other ingredients. Stir. Continue cooking until all ingredients are tender.
Per Serving:
Calories—185; Total Fat—4%; Sat. Fat—0.049 g; Choles.—0; Fiber—2.8 g

TUNA SALAD
4 Servings

6 ounces of tuna packed in water
½ cup low-fat yogurt
½ celery stalk, chopped

1 small onion, chopped
1 tsp. lemon juice
½ tsp. Dijon mustard

Drain tuna. Combine tuna with yogurt and other ingredients. Serve as desired.

Per Serving:
Calories—82.6; Total Fat—15%; Sat. Fat—0.29 g; Choles.—17.9 mg; Fiber—1 g

SPICE COOKIES
60 Cookies

½ cup sugar
⅔ cup soft margarine
1 cup molasses
½ cup water
2 cups whole-wheat flour

1 tsp. allspice
1 tsp. ginger
1 tsp. ground cloves
1 tsp. cinnamon
1½ tsp. baking soda

Preheat oven to 375° F. Cream sugar and margarine. Beat in molasses and water. Combine flour, spices and baking soda in a separate bowl. Stir into the molasses mixture. Keep stirring until batter is thin and smooth. Drop in 1-Tbsp. amounts onto a nonstick cookie sheet. Bake for 8 to 10 minutes.

Per Cookie:
Calories—48; Total Fat—24%; Sat. Fat—0.19 g; Choles.—0; Fiber—2 g

YOGURT DRESSING
12 Servings

½ cup low-fat plain yogurt
2 Tbsp. lemon juice
1 Tbsp. soy sauce

1 tsp. Dijon mustard
1 tsp. parsley, chopped

Combine all ingredients in a blender and blend until smooth. Serve immediately.

Per Serving:
Calories—7.9; Total Fat—19%; Sat. Fat—0.09 g; Choles.—0.58 mg; Fiber—0

BANANA SHAKE
2 Servings

½ cup low-fat plain yogurt
1 cup low-fat milk

2 bananas, chopped
¼ tsp. cinnamon
1 tsp. vanilla

Combine all ingredients in a blender and blend until smooth. Serve immediately.

Per Serving:
Calories—196.8; Total Fat—13%; Sat. Fat—1.6 g; Choles.—8.5 mg; Fiber—2.8 g

Marti Shohet

The

LOW-FAT DINNER

Dinner is a meal at which you can control the food your children eat. Keep these two thoughts in mind when you're planning dinners.

Stephen Osborn

- Low-fat dinners can be attractive, varied and tasty.
- Healthy, nutritious meals can be prepared quickly and easily. Plan your dinners around low-fat entrees. Serve turkey and chicken (without the skin) and fish and shellfish (except shrimp) often.

Vegetables contribute vitamins, minerals, dietary fiber and energy-giving starches. They should be varied frequently. Two servings at dinner are recommended. Considering the wide variety of vegetables that are available all year, you should be able to find quite a few that your family likes.

Cook vegetables by steaming or microwave heating to retain nutrients. The less you do to vegetables, the less fattening they are. Strive for fresh or frozen vegetables instead of canned varieties.

Don't forget the potato, a vegetable that's been wrongly associated with being overweight. An average potato that's boiled or baked has no more calories than an apple or a pear. And far from being pure starch, the potato has protein, calcium, iron and vitamin C. It also has almost no fat. It's what people do to potatoes that makes them fatty. French-fried, scalloped, home-fried, or mashed potatoes with butter and milk have fat added and should be avoided.

Consider serving meatless meals several times a week. You can provide adequate protein with beans, chick peas, lentils, enriched pastas, whole grains, and vegetables. Dried beans of all kinds are tasty, rich in fiber and protein, and very low in fat. They can be the basis for several meatless meals. Numerous meatless pasta dishes, such as vegetable lasagna and spaghetti with marinara sauce, are low-fat, tasty and nutritious.

From time to time, have stir-fried dinners. These are made of thinly sliced vegetables and a small amount of meat cooked quickly in a tiny amount of vegetable oil and served with rice.

Children should have salad greens frequently. Boston, bibb and romaine lettuce, watercress, endive, kale, chicory, and radicchio are good sources of vitamins A and C.

Adjust your cooking methods to keep fat out of food in these ways:

- Avoid frying meat, fish and poultry. Instead, roast, bake, braise, broil, grill, poach or stir-fry.
- Use low roasting temperatures (325° to 350°F) to increase the fat drip-off.
- Skim the fat off cooking liquid when braising or stewing.
- When broiling, use a rack so that fat can drip off.
- Trim visible fat from meats.
- Avoid deep-fat frying of food.
- Use vegetable-oil sprays instead of margarine or butter in frying pans.

Nina Wallace

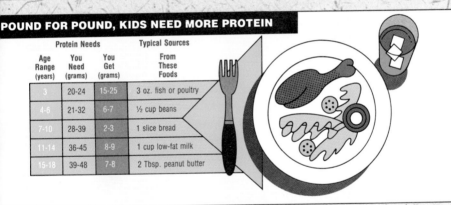

POUND FOR POUND, KIDS NEED MORE PROTEIN

| | Protein Needs | | Typical Sources |
Age Range (years)	You Need (grams)	You Get (grams)	From These Foods
3	20-24	15-25	3 oz. fish or poultry
4-6	21-32	6-7	½ cup beans
7-10	28-39	2-3	1 slice bread
11-14	36-45	8-9	1 cup low-fat milk
15-18	39-48	7-8	2 Tbsp. peanut butter

PROTEIN

For many years, protein was the hero of the American food scene. People thought that if you ate a lot of protein, you were on the road to endless good health. Animal products, such as meat, poultry, fish, eggs, milk and cheese, are high in protein. But they are also often high in saturated fat and cholesterol. Many plant foods, such as dry beans, grains and cereals, also contain a lot of protein, but not a lot of fat.

Nuts and seeds are important sources of protein, but most are high in monounsaturated fat.

As valuable and indispensable as protein is, most of us don't need as much as we think we need.

Growing children need more protein, in proportion to their weight, than do adults. Pregnant women need more than other female adults do.

Stephen Osborn

Seven LOW-FAT DINNER IDEAS

1

London broil
Orange-glazed carrots*
Mashed potatoes
Lettuce and tomato salad
French bread
Baked apple
1 cup low-fat milk

2

Chicken cutlets with spinach
Oven-fried potato with skin
Spinach
Chicory-orange salad*
1 percent-fat milk

3

Baked scrod with bread crumbs*
Steamed spinach
Carrot-nut salad
Roll
Tropical fruit cup
1 cup low-fat milk

4

Stuffed turkey breast without skin*
Noodles
Steamed peas
Baked stuffed squash
Ice milk and strawberries
Lemonade

5

Spaghetti with T-T sauce*
Green beans
Salad with lemon herb dressing
Italian bread
Milk-based (low-fat) pudding
Fruit spritzer

6

Ground turkey meatloaf
Mixed vegetables with rice
Cucumber salad
Whole-wheat rolls
Angel food cake
1 cup low-fat milk

7

Roast chicken
Sweet potato
Baked tomato
Citrus salad
Lemon rice pudding
Hot spiced cider

Low-Fat
DINNER RECIPES

STUFFED TURKEY BREAST   *4 Servings*

2 lbs. boneless turkey breast
8-ounce can sliced water chestnuts
10 ounces sliced mushrooms
1 bunch scallions
1 cup low-fat plain yogurt

2 Tbsp. tomato paste
2 Tbsp. lemon juice
2 Tbsp. sesame seeds

Preheat oven to 350° F. Mix water chestnuts, mushrooms and scallions. In another bowl, mix yogurt, tomato paste and lemon juice. Combine three quarters of the dressing mixture with vegetables. Place a heaping table-spoon of vegetable sauce mixture into the middle of the turkey breast. Roll up turkey and place on rack in baking pan. Top with remaining vegetables, dressing mixture and sesame seeds. Roast for 45 minutes.

Per Serving:
Calories—270; Total Fat—15%; Sat. Fat—0.88 g; Choles.—98 mg; Fiber—1.4 g

ORANGE GLAZED CARROTS   *6 Servings*

8 large carrots, cut thin, diagonally
¼ cup orange juice
1 tsp. margarine

2 Tbsp. sliced mandarin orange
1 Tbsp. mustard

Combine margarine and orange juice in a saucepan and simmer. Add carrot slices and simmer until tender, but still crisp. Add mustard and oranges. Serve immediately.

Per Serving:
Calories—57; Total Fat—16%; Sat. Fat—0.142 g; Choles.—0; Fiber—2.9 g

BAKED SCROD WITH TOPPING

6 *Servings*

2 lbs. scrod, boned
1 cup white bread-crumbs

2 Tbsp. melted margarine
1 tsp. Tabasco sauce
1 tsp. powdered bouillon

Preheat oven to 350° F. Mix crumbs with margarine, Tabasco Sauce and bouillon. Place fish on a baking sheet. Pat crumb mixture over each portion. Bake for 15 minutes. Finish cooking under a broiler to brown the crumbs.

Per Serving:
Calories—190; Total Fat—26%; Sat. Fat—0.69 g; Choles.—0.01 mg; Fiber—1 g

CHICORY-ORANGE SALAD WITH WATERCRESS DRESSING

6 *Servings*

3 heads chicory, washed
2 oranges, peeled
2 bunches watercress, chopped
2 Tbsp. low-fat yogurt

1 tsp. Dijon mustard
3 Tbsp. tarragon vinegar
or white vinegar
Salt and pepper

Cut chicory into small pieces. Slice oranges thinly across sections, then cut into half-circle slices. Mix chicory and oranges in a salad bowl. Mix together vinegar, mustard, pepper, salt and watercress and pour into yogurt to make dressing.

Per Serving:
Calories—67; Total Fat—9%; Sat. Fat—0.154 g; Choles.—0.29 mg; Fiber—4.4 g

SPAGHETTI WITH T-T SAUCE

6 *Servings*

1 lb. cooked spaghetti
1 can tuna in water, drained
½ cup cooked peas
½ cup chopped onion
4 large ripe tomatoes or
6 plum tomatoes, peeled,
cut into chunks

½ Tbsp. olive oil
¼ cup tomato purée
½ Tbsp. basil
½ Tbsp. thyme
Dash of coriander
Fresh ground pepper
1 Tbsp. Parmesan cheese

Blend tomato chunks and tomato purée with spices. Sauté onions in olive oil until golden. Add tomato sauce, tuna and peas and simmer 5 to 10 minutes. Mix with spaghetti and serve with a light sprinkle of Parmesan cheese on top.

Per Serving:
Calories—204; Total Fat—13%; Sat. Fat—0.41 g; Choles.—11.6 mg; Fiber—2.9 g

Marti Shohet

DINING OUT

Stephen Osborn

You don't have to leave your new, healthy eating habits at home when you decide to eat out. It's possible for your family to eat low-fat restaurant meals that are appealing and delicious. Just apply the same rules you use for healthy eating at home to restaurant dining. Believe it or not, you can follow these rules without taking the fun from eating out. The younger your children are, the easier it is. For children young enough to rely on you to order the meal, there's not much to it. If your children are old enough to want to order their own food, it helps to have some calm talks about the dangers of high-fat food. Show them how to politely request low-fat choices, such as broiled instead of fried chicken and baked instead of French-fried potatoes.

Because of growing interest in healthful eating, most restaurants are now used to special requests. Many offer special low-calorie meals. When you know what to watch out for and how to make simple changes, it's easy to eat out pleasantly and sensibly.

DINING-OUT CHOICES

Order Often	Order Rarely
Appetizers	
fruit cocktail	antipasto
raw vegetables	jumbo shrimp cocktail
melon	French-fried onion rings
Soups	
broth with noodles	cream soups
minestrone	cheese soup
Entrees	
fish, chicken, turkey	fatty cuts of meat
lean meats that are broiled,	goose, duck, hot dogs, omelettes,
baked, steamed or boiled	hamburgers, anything that has
	"Parmigiana" in its name.
Vegetables	
all varieties steamed,	all varieties with butter or cream
baked or boiled potatoes	sauce, French fries, hash-
	brown potatoes, home fries
Salads	
mixed greens, tomatoes,	egg salad, chicken salad, salads
cucumbers with oil and	with creamy dressing
vinegar	
Beverages	
skim or low-fat milk, juices,	whole milk, milk shake, malted
club soda, seltzer	milk, soda
Desserts	
Fresh fruit, angel food cake,	Cake, pie, cheesecake, ice cream,
sherbet, Jello	éclairs, puddings, pastries

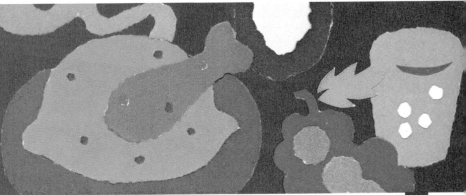

Here are some guidelines for low-fat restaurant dining:

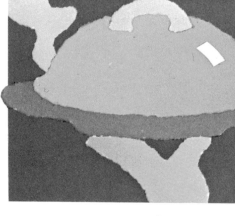

- Order a la carte, instead of the entire dinner. That way, you won't be faced with dishes you don't really want or need and yet feel you must eat because you paid for them.
- If a vegetable relish tray is offered, eat the vegetables and avoid the creamy dips.
- Stay away from creamy appetizers and cream soups.
- When ordering salad, ask for the dressing on the side and use only the amount you want. A healthy dressing is olive oil and vinegar or lemon juice. If there's a salad bar, skip the bacon bits and the cheese crumbles.
- Order meat and fish broiled, baked, steamed or roasted, but not fried or sautéed. When ordering beef, remember that those tender steaks are tender because so much fat is mixed in with the meat. London broil is a wiser choice.
- Limit gravies and cream, cheese and butter sauces. Ask for these on the side, if at all.
- Ask for vegetables steamed or plain.
- Potatoes with skin, rice, and pastas are recommended. Keep the butter or cream toppings to a minimum.
- Low-fat dessert possibilities are angel food cake, meringue, sherbets, Italian ices, ice milk, and fresh fruit.

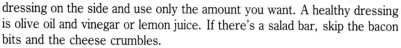

MAKE YOUR CHILD'S MENU HEALTHIER

Instead of	Choose
spaghetti with meatballs	spaghetti with marinara sauce
roll and butter	roll plain or with margarine
ice cream	sherbet
milk or cola	1 percent-fat milk or fruit juice
fried filet of sole	broiled filet of sole
French fries	mashed potatoes
cole slaw	lettuce and tomato slices
custard	fruit salad
milk	juice
roast beef	ask for lean cut
vegetables	_____
mashed potatoes	_____
roll and butter	roll plain or with margarine
ice cream sundae	sherbet
milk or soda	1 percent-fat milk
chopped sirloin steak	roast turkey
vegetables	_____
mashed potatoes and gravy	omit the gravy
ice cream	melon
milk or cola	1 percent-fat milk

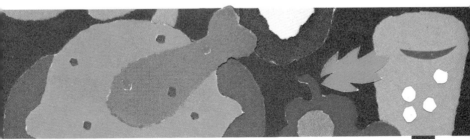

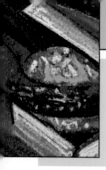

LIFE IN THE FAST-FOOD LANE

Stephen Osborn

Americans spend $50 billion a year in fast-food restaurants. Most of that money goes for such fatty foods as hamburgers, cheeseburgers, fried chicken, hot dogs, French fries and milk shakes.

The prevalence and popularity of fast-food restaurants make them difficult to avoid. Children in particular are attracted to them.

However, the fast-food restaurant scene need not be avoided at all costs. Informed consumers can find healthful options for themselves and their children. Some fast-food restaurants are making an effort to offer some nutritious low-fat food choices. Become aware of those choices and the restaurants that are offering them.

A few fast-food restaurants still use beef tallow, a saturated fat, for frying. Many others, however, are switching to healthier vegetable oil.

Marti Shohet

Some now provide salad bars and offer 1 percent-fat or skim milk, fruit juices and ready-to-serve cereals for breakfast.

Fast-food restaurants are never likely to win three cheers from your children's arteries. But it is possible to find reasonably healthy food in most of them.

SALAD BARS

Choose raw vegetables, beans and fresh fruit, which have little fat and are high in vitamins A and C and in fiber. Avoid the fat-laden dressings. The macaroni salad and potato salad may be full of mayonnaise.

T. Starrett

FISH

Several chains offer healthful baked fish. If only deep-fried fish is available, you can make it healthier by removing the fatty, crispy coating it's been fried in. Skip the tartar sauce. You can use red or cocktail sauce instead.

CHICKEN

Several chains offer baked or broiled chicken parts, which make good low-fat choices. Beware of chicken nuggets. They are made of processed chicken, including ground skin. If fried chicken parts are the only choice, encourage your child to pick away the crispy coating and skin.

PIZZA

Despite its cheese, plain pizza is a fairly well-balanced food that can be relatively low in fat. Try to avoid toppings such as pepperoni, sausage, meatballs and extra cheese. Good alternative toppings are peppers, onions, extra sauce and mushrooms.

HAMBURGERS

Eating a hamburger from time to time won't damage your children's health. Encourage them to choose the smaller, plain, well-done hamburgers and not patties with cheese and bacon. Lettuce and tomato make a healthy topping.

POTATOES

Most French fries are still cooked in deep vats of beef tallow. Baked potatoes are a much better choice. Avoid creamy and cheesy toppings. If available, try alternate toppings such as low-fat salad dressing or taco sauce.

BEVERAGES

Milk shakes and malted milks are loaded with fat and cholesterol. One percent-fat milk, fruit juice, and water are better choices.

DESSERTS

Try to skip the desserts, unless fruit and sherbet are available.

DESSERT

LOW-FAT SNACKS

Stephen Osborn

Snacking is a part of children's lives. Even though they may not learn it at home, children are bound to pick up the habit when they go to school. The best way to cope with snacking is to make low-fat, appetizing snacks available at home. Give your children a taste for healthy food that they can follow when they're out in the world.

There are hundreds of snacks and drinks that will do your children's hearts good.

The classic after-school snack is a glass of milk and peanut butter and bread. Make that skim or low-fat milk and some whole-wheat or whole-grain bread and you've done something nice for a child's arteries.

OFF THE TREE AND FAT-FREE

The healthiest snacks are fruits and raw vegetables. They are almost fat-free and completely cholesterol-free.

A bowl with three or more kinds of fruit on the kitchen table will attract

children's attention. Encourage your children to wash and eat the skins of fruits when possible. Most of the fiber and vitamins in fruits are found in and just under the skin.

You can prevent sliced fruit from turning brown and also add extra flavoring by squeezing lemon, lime or orange juice on it.

Try dried fruits, such as raisins, figs, apricots, dates and prunes.

GARDEN GEMS

Fresh vegetables gain crispness and crunchiness if you soak them in icy water before serving.

Marti Shohet

Reduce the Fat in Cookies

An oatmeal cookie recipe can be changed to greatly reduce fat, cholesterol, and calories.

Ingredients for Typical Oatmeal Cookies

	Calories	Fat (g)	Sat. fat (g)	Choles. (mg)
Flour, white–1 cup	420	1.00	0.20	0.0
Sugar, white–½ cup	360	0.00	0.00	0.0
Oatmeal, cooked– 2 cups	290	4.80	0.88	0.0
Shortening, veg.– ⅓ cup	598	67.65	16.90	0.0
Eggs, 2	158	11.16	3.34	548.0
Milk, whole–¼ cup	38	2.04	1.28	8.3
Raisins, seedless– ½ cup	217	0.34	0.11	0.0
Baking soda–½ tsp.	0	0.00	0.00	0.0
Cinnamon–¼ tsp.	1	0.02	0.00	0.0
Total	**2,082**	**87.00**	**22.69**	**556.3**

Ingredients for Modified Oatmeal Cookies

	Calories	Fat (g)	Sat. fat (g)	Choles. (mg)
Flour, whole wheat– 1 cup	400	2.00	0.40	0.0
Sugar, white–½ cup	360	0.00	0.00	0.0
Oatmeal, cooked– 2 cups	290	4.80	0.88	0.0
Milk, skim–¼ cup	22	0.11	0.07	1.0
Raisins, seedless– ½ cup	217	0.34	0.11	0.0
Baking soda– ½ tsp.	0	0.00	0.00	0.0
Cinnamon–¼ tsp.	1	0.02	0.00	0.0
Total	**1,290**	**7.27**	**1.46**	**1.0**

Preparation Method for Modified Oatmeal Cookies

Preheat oven to 375°F. Mix sugar, milk and cooked oatmeal. In a separate bowl, mix flour, baking soda and cinnamon. Stir the flour mixture and the oatmeal mixture in a large bowl. Add raisins while stirring. Shape the mixture into individual cookies and place on cookie sheet. Bake for 10 minutes. The yield should be about three dozen cookies.

T. Starrett

With a few exceptions, fresh, raw vegetables make appetizing, healthy snacks. For snacking, choose vegetables that are firm, clean and unblemished. Small cucumbers, green beans, carrots and celery are more tender than large pieces.

Be adventurous. Cauliflower, broccoli, turnips, mushrooms, green peppers, tiny onions, radishes, celery, pickles, bean sprouts and tomato slices make colorful, attractive snacks.

GOING WITH THE GRAIN

Breads, crackers and even breakfast cereals can make for varied and healthy snacks. Whole-grain breads and cereals provide vitamins, minerals and fiber, and they have very little saturated fat. When buying whole-grain bread, make sure that the label lists whole grain as the first ingredient.

For spreads, instead of butter or margarine use low-fat ricotta cheese, cottage cheese, peanut butter, humus, jams and jellies, sliced cucumber or sliced bananas.

Whole-grain beakfast cereals without added fat can be put out in a bowl to be eaten like popcorn or served with low-fat milk and fruit in the conventional way.

Air-popped or microwaved popcorn without butter is a good snack.

Nuts are healthy, nutritious snacks, full of protein. They contain fat, but very little of it is saturated fat. Nuts make good snacks in moderation.

BAKED GOODS

When making muffins, cookies or cakes, substitute whole-wheat flour for half the white flour, or use all whole-wheat. Check the consistency of the whole-wheat batter. You may need to add liquid to keep the batter moist.

If you serve cakes and muffins with a topping, try a thin spread of low-fat ricotta or cottage cheese instead of butter or margarine.

When buying baked goods, avoid products high in saturated fat, cholesterol and added sugar. Try to buy whole-wheat, bran or corn muffins and cookies and cakes made from whole-wheat flour.

PARTY SNACKS

All the different kinds of packaged snacks available have three things in common: they are fatty, salty, and crunchy.

Crunchiness is great.

A lot of salt isn't so good because it can cause high blood pressure.

Fatty is bad news. Potato chips, corn chips, cheese puffs, tortilla chips and most of the other munchies are heavy in fat.

Pretzels have salt and crunch, but little fat. Other low-fat crunchy snacks include puffed cereals with powdered seasonings, low-fat crackers, carrot sticks and celery sticks with low-fat cheese, humus and low-fat yogurt dips.

SNACKING AWAY FROM HOME

The younger your children are, the easier it will be to make low-fat eating a lifetime habit that they will take with them wherever they go. Once your children are old enough to go to school by themselves, you've got to rely on their good sense about the things they eat.

Teenagers need gentle handling in eating matters. Explain the dangers of too much fat and the wisdom of avoiding fat. Tell them how they can eat sensibly among their friends without appearing to be different. Try not to give orders about what not to eat, and don't bring up the subject frequently. Praise good eating habits. Let your teenagers know you love them and want them to be around for a long time.

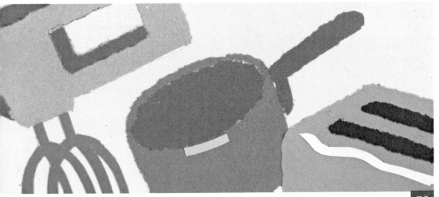

Stephen Osborn

Low-Fat
SNACK RECIPES

CAMP-OUT SNACK MIX

5 Servings

5 cups cereal, Crispix
¼ cup raisins
¼ cup peanuts

¼ cup sunflower seeds
¼ cup diced dates or prunes

Combine all ingredients. Store tightly covered or in individual plastic bags.

Per Serving:
Calories—232; Total Fat—27%; Sat. Fat—0.85 g; Choles.—0; Fiber—2.3 g

APPLE-CARROT MUFFINS

36 Muffins

3 cups whole-wheat flour
1 cup rolled oats (oatmeal)
1½ tsp. baking powder
½ tsp. nutmeg
½ tsp. allspice
1 tsp. cinnamon

½ cup sugar
1 cup grated carrot
1 cup grated apple (unpeeled)
2 cups buttermilk (low-fat)
2 egg whites
1 tsp. polyunsaturated oil

Preheat oven to 400° F.

Mix dry ingredients. Fold in grated carrot and apple. Combine eggs, buttermilk and oil, and stir into dry mixture. Pour into lightly oiled or nonstick muffin tins and bake for 20-25 minutes.

Per Muffin:
Calories—63; Total Fat—7%; Sat. Fat—0.09 g; Choles.—0; Fiber—1.6 g

Marti Shohet

MILKY WAY

6 Servings

1 quart skim milk
3 cups orange juice

½ tsp. cinnamon
⅓ cup lemon juice
1 Tbsp. honey (optional)

Blend ingredients.

Per Serving:
Calories—117; Total Fat—4%; Sat. Fat—0.22 g; Choles.—2.667 mg; Fiber—1 g

FRUITY ICE

4 Servings

2 peeled oranges
2 peeled bananas
2 cups crushed ice

2 cups apple sauce,
  unsweetened
½ tsp. cinnamon

Mix ingredients in blender, adding ice slowly.

Per Serving:
Calories—139; Total Fat—3%; Sat. Fat—0.13 g; Choles.—0; Fiber—4.77 g

CEREAL SUNDAE

2 Servings

1 cup low-fat yogurt or low-fat milk
½ cup sliced fresh or cooked fruit

½ cup toasted wheat germ
  or uncooked oatmeal
1 Tbsp. sunflower seeds

Combine or layer ingredients in a parfait dish.

Per Serving:
Calories—221; Total Fat—29%; Sat. Fat—1.9 g; Choles.—7 mg; Fiber—2.6 g

CINNAMON-APPLE CRUNCH

12 Servings

5 cups cereal
¼ cup walnut halves
¼ cup sugar

½ tsp. ground cinnamon
½ cup coarsely cut
  dried apples

Combine cereal and walnuts in 13″ x 9″ x 2″ baking pan.

Stir together sugar and cinnamon. Sprinkle over cereal mixture, stirring to coat evenly.

Bake at 250° F. for 45 minutes, stirring every 15 minutes. Gently stir in apples. Spread on absorbent paper to cool.

Yield: about 6 cups.

Per Serving:
Calories— 84; Total Fat—17%; Sat. Fat—0.10 g; Choles.—0; Fiber—0.2 g

A New Awareness

Many families are making healthy, low-fat eating patterns a priority. That's normal. Talk about healthy eating with your children to head off their feelings of being different. Occasionally, kids may feel out of step when they choose sherbet instead of ice cream, or salads instead of chili dogs. A positive attitude toward low-fat, low-cholesterol eating at home can enable them to weather such "storms." In a quiet way, without being preachy, your children's good eating habits can influence others.

Of course, children go through stages in the process of growing up. The independent assertion, "No, I don't want that," reflects a common stage. Another stage consists of wanting to eat the same type of food meal after meal. This may be accompanied or followed by certain food "phobias"—aversions to peas, fish or spinach, for instance.

The best way to deal with these stages is not to make a big issue out of them. At the same time, continue to serve a variety of nutritious, low-fat foods. The stages pass, but the healthy eating patterns that are set at home will last a lifetime.

GLOSSARY

Atherosclerosis: The term comes from two Greek words: *athere*, which means porridge, and *sklerosis*, which means hardening. It describes the buildup of fatty deposits on the inner layers of artery walls, causing a narrowing and hardening of the arteries.

Calorie: The fuel value of food is expressed in calories. In general terms, one calorie is the amount of heat energy needed to raise the temperature of one gram of water 1° C. In nutritional terms, it is the equivalent amount of energy produced when food is oxidized, or burned, in the body.

Carbohydrates: Various compounds of carbon, hydrogen and oxygen in the form of sugars, starches and celluloses. Simple carbohydrates include sugars from cane, sugar beets, corn syrup, milk and fruit. Complex carbohydrates include the starches found in whole grain, cereals, breads, pasta and potatoes.

Cholesterol: A fatlike substance needed by the body to help cells grow. Cholesterol is unhealthy only when a person's blood contains too much of it.

Dietary Fiber: The part of grains, fruits, vegetables, beans and nuts that humans cannot digest. It includes substances, such as cellulose, hemicellulose and lignin, that do not dissolve in water. It also includes substances, such as gum and pectin, that do dissolve in water. Research suggests that water-insoluble fiber helps move food through the digestive tract and may prevent some types of cancer.

Fats: Like carbohydrates, fats are made up of compounds of carbon, hydrogen and oxygen. Food fats provide more food energy calories per gram than protein or carbohydrates.

Hydrogenated Fat: The addition of hydrogen to vegetable oils during processing can make the substances solid or semisolid and give them longer shelf life. However, hydrogenation converts some of the unsaturated fat in the product to saturated fat.

Monounsaturated Fat: Fat in certain plant and animal foods that may lower blood cholesterol. Olive oil is rich in monounsaturated fatty acids.

Polyunsaturated Fat: Fat, usually of vegetable origin, that is liquid at room temperature. Safflower and sunflower oils are rich in polyunsaturated fatty acids. Polyunsaturated fat may lower blood cholesterol.

Saturated Fat: Fat that is usually solid at room temperature and is mostly of animal origin. Typical sources are cheese, butter, lard and meat fat.

Sources of
MORE INFORMATION

To help you control fat and cholesterol in your family's diet, the following national organizations may provide further information in the form of educational materials, books, booklets, nutrition counseling and cooking classes.

American Health Foundation
320 East 43rd Street
New York, New York 10017
(212) 953-1900

American Heart Association
7330 Greenville Avenue
Dallas, Texas 75231
(214) 750-5300

Food and Nutrition Information
National Agricultural Library
NAL Building, Room 304
10301 Baltimore Boulevard
Beltsville, Maryland 20705
(301) 344-3719

Human Nutrition Information
Service
Public Information Office
Room 360, Federal Building
6506 Belcrest Road
Hyattsville, Maryland 20782
(301) 436-8617

National Cholesterol Education
Program
C-200, Suite 530
4733 Bethesda Avenue
Bethesda, Maryland 20814
(301) 951-3260

Various local organizations also provide nutrition information, references and services. Some may be in a position to answer individual queries and to conduct local projects such as nutrition fairs, lectures, and low-fat, low-cholesterol cooking classes.

For information on local resources, contact:
- **Your Local Dietetic Assocation or Consultation Service**
- **Your School System Adult Education Department**
- **Your County, City or Local Health Departments**
- **Your Universities and Colleges**

THE SHOPPING GUIDE

You can greatly reduce the fat in family meals by seeking low-fat options for the food items you normally buy. Here are examples of lower-fat choices that can be made right at the shopping cart.

INSTEAD OF	BUY
egg noodles	spaghetti
croissant	bagel
ice cream	sherbet
sour cream	plain low-fat yogurt
regular ground beef	very lean ground beef
bacon strip	Canadian bacon
cream cheese	low-fat cottage cheese
bologna, salami	turkey bologna, turkey breast
beef hot dog	turkey/chicken hot dog
cinnamon roll	English muffin with jam
pork chop	pork tenderloin
lamb chop	leg of lamb
potato chips	air-popped popcorn
mayonnaise	diet mayonnaise
chocolate cake	angel food cake
chocolate chip cookies	gingersnap cookies
regular salad dressing	diet salad dressing
creamy dip	spicy sauce
peanuts	chestnuts
corn chips	pretzels
vanilla sandwich cookies	fig bars
dark meat chicken with skin	light meat chicken, no skin
fried chicken leg	roasted chicken breast
ice cream pop	frozen fruit pop
powdered nondairy coffee creamer	nonfat dry milk

To further assist you to make low-fat, low-cholesterol food shopping choices, the following pages list fat and cholesterol content of many frequently purchased food items.

Fats & Cholesterol
IN THE FOODS WE EAT

	Serving Size	Total Fat (g)	Saturated Fat (g)	Cholesterol (mg)
MEAT				
Beef				
hamburger, *broiled*				
regular	3 oz.	18	7	76
lean	3 oz.	16	6	74
chuck, *braised and simmered*	3 oz.	26	11	87
round, *regular cut*	3 oz.	13	5	69
steak, *fatty cut, broiled*	3 oz.	16	7	67
steak, *lean, broiled*	3 oz.	8	3	64
beef and bean burrito	1 oz.	17	7	52
beef taco	1 oz.	11	4	21
roast beef sandwich	1 oz.	13	4	55
liver, *fried*	2 oz.	6	29	250
Bacon, *cooked crisp*	2 slices	8	3	14
Frankfurter (10 per lb.)				
beef and pork	1	13	5	23
turkey	1	8	2	44
chicken	1	9	3	45
Bologna	1 oz.	8	3	16
POULTRY				
Chicken				
breast, *fried, batter-dipped*	½	9	3	60
breast, *roasted without skin*	½	3	1	73
roll, *light meat*	2 oz.	4	1	28
Turkey, *roasted*				
white meat, *no skin*	3 oz.	3	1	60
dark meat, *no skin*	3 oz.	6	2	72
Ham luncheon meat	1 oz.	6	2	13
FISH & EGGS				
Tuna fish				
water-packed	3 oz.	trace	trace	15
oil-packed	3 oz.	7	1	15
tuna salad	½ cup	10	3	40

	Serving Size	Total Fat (g)	Saturated Fat (g)	Cholesterol (mg)
Flounder or sole, *baked w/o fat*	3 oz.	1	trace	58
Salmon, *baked w/o fat*	3 oz.	9	2	74
Shrimp, *boiled, no shells*	3½ oz.	1	trace	195
Eggs, *large raw*				
whole	1	6	2	274
yolk only	1	6	2	274
white only	1	trace	0	0

POTATOES

Baked, *whole or sweet*	1 med.	trace	trace	0
French-fried	10 strips	8	3	0
Chips	14	10	3	0
Au gratin	½ cup	19	12	56
Salad with mayonnaise and egg	½ cup	11	2	85

VEGETABLES AND BEANS

Cabbage coleslaw	1 cup	3	1	10
All other vegetables, *raw or cooked without fat*	1 cup	trace	trace	0
Soybeans, *cooked from dry*	1 cup	15	2	0
Tofu	½ cup	6	1	0
Refried beans, *canned*	1 cup	3	1	0
Garbanzo beans, *cooked*	1 cup	4	trace	0
Baked beans, *canned with pork*	1 cup	3	1	17

FRUITS

Avocado	½ med.	15	2	0
Olives, *ripe*	5 large	5	1	0
Olives, *green*	5 large	3	trace	0
Coconut, *shredded*	1 cup	28	24	0
All other fruits, *w/o added fat*	½-1 cup	trace	trace	0

GRAIN PRODUCTS

Bread, *made w/o eggs*	1 slice	1	trace	0
Oatmeal, *cooked*	1 cup	2	trace	0
Whole-wheat cereal, *cooked*	1 cup	1	trace	0
Dry breakfast cereals	1 cup	trace	trace	0
Granola, *homemade*	1 cup	33	6	0
Popcorn, *airpopped, plain*	1 cup	trace	trace	0
Popcorn, *popped in veg. oil*	1 cup	3	1	0
Rice, pasta, *cooked*	1 cup	1	trace	0
Egg noodles, *cooked*	1 cup	2	1	50

	Serving Size	Total Fat (g)	Saturated Fat (g)	Cholesterol (mg)
FATS AND OILS				
Butter	1 Tbsp.	11	7	31
Margarine, *stick or tub*	1 Tbsp.	11	2	0
tub	1 Tbsp.	11	2	0
Oils:				
soybean or safflower	1 Tbsp.	11	14	0
sunflower, corn, or olive	1 Tbsp.	14	0	
peanut	1 Tbsp.	14	2	0
Mayonnaise	1 Tbsp.	11	2	8
French salad dressing	1 Tbsp.	9	1	0
SWEETS				
Milk chocolate candy	1 oz.	9	5	6
Chocolate fudge candy	1 oz.	3	2	1
Marshmallows	4 large	0	0	0
Hard candy, *all flavors*	1 oz.	0	0	0
Jelly beans	1 oz.	trace	trace	0
Chocolate syrup, *thin*	2 Tbsp.	trace	trace	0
Chocolate syrup, *thick*	2 Tbsp.	5	3	0
Pancake syrup	2 Tbsp.	0	0	0
Sugars, *white or brown*	1 tsp.	0	0	0
DAIRY FOOD				
Cream:				
Half & half	1 Tbsp.	2	1	6
Light, *for whipping*	1 Tbsp.	5	3	17
Heavy	1 Tbsp.	6	3.5	20
Whipped, *in pressure can*	2 Tbsp.	2	1	6
Sour cream	1 Tbsp.	3	2	6
Dessert topping, *frozen*	2 Tbsp.	2	2	0
Dessert topping, *pressure can*	2 Tbsp.	2	1	1
MILK				
Whole	1 cup	8	5	33
2% fat	1 cup	5	3	22
1% fat	1 cup	3	1.5	10
Skim	1 cup	1	.3	4
Buttermilk	1 cup	2	1.3	9
Evaporated milk, *whole*	½ cup	10	6	37
Sweetened condensed milk	½ cup	13.5	8.5	52